CHRONICLES OF LIFE

IN *Poetry*

Reviews

There's only one word to describe the feeling that the poems have evoked in me, 'soothing'. They remind me of the series *Chicken Soup for the Soul*. These poems carry a lot of heartwarming messages and they make good reading for one with a worn out body and a burnout state of mind. They depict life's journey and most importantly, the poet's own journey through life and his views about matters that affect him. The language used is simple yet meaningful. The choice of words is apt and conveys the message that the poet wished to express most vividly. I can relate to the poem *Say It* as we constantly forget the healing power of words. Both poems *Thankful* and *Everything's Great* share a similar message i.e., on the importance of being appreciative no matter how unkind or unjustly we are treated. Life is what we made out of it and if we choose to be a pessimist, then we will constantly see things in a bad light. On the whole, *Chronicles of Life in Poetry* will be a splendid collection as the messages are filled with many life's touching moments—pleasures and melancholies.

Yong Lee Choo
Institute of Teacher Education
Technical Education Campus
Bandar Enstek, Negeri Sembilan, Malaysia

The poet deals with an array of situations in life which I can easily identify with. His choice of words aptly demonstrates his unique ability to negotiate and discuss issues using connotations that only poetry lovers can unravel. The anthology is a reassuring read with heaps of motivational words and the hope of staying vigilant against all odds in this vicious world of substance as illustrated in *Keep me up*. *Everything's great* is about the need for self-reflections in bliss and agony as a way forward. All in all, this compendium of poetries which touches on a wide range of daily tussles and the fair hope of victory over mind-boggling situations would surely enhance the readers' understanding of the multifaceted scope of real life experiences.

Assoc. Prof. Dr. Rosli Talif
Department of English
Faculty of Modern Languages and Communication
Universiti Putra Malaysia

CHRONICLES OF LIFE

IN *Poetry*

ADRIAN WEE KOK SENG

For book orders, email orders@traffordpublishing.com.sg

Most Trafford Singapore titles are also available at major online book retailers.

Printed in Singapore.

ISBN: 978-1-4669-9148-4 (sc)
ISBN: 978-1-4669-9147-7 (e)

Trafford rev. 05/22/2013

 www.traffordpublishing.com.sg

Singapore
toll-free: 800 101 2656 (Singapore)
Fax: 800 101 2656 (Singapore)

Contents

Preface

With the gift of words and ideas to write almost spontaneously, my love for poetry-writing grew. It started with my pure interest in expressing my views about my personal encounters in life.

It all began as a new voyage for me when I realized that there is so much to share about living strong and not submitting the self to unnecessary tribulations and miseries. It is my earnest desire to help as many troubled individuals to understand life's tests and see the light at the end of the tunnel.

One key to living strong, is found in Adlai Stevenson's and William Jennings Bryan's quotes, "It is not the years in your life but the life in your years that counts" and "Destiny is not a matter of chance, it is a matter of choice; it is not a thing to be waited for, it is a thing to be achieved." These convey strong connotations about the significance of enjoying quality life and making the right choices for a comfortable life in the future.

This collection of poems incorporate many different strokes of life that will propagate positive awareness that we are all winners, not born losers as many had believed. Remember that true happiness does not depend on wealth and success but by the way we think and live which further influence our spoken words and actions.

On the whole, this anthology of poems is all authentic and they are the selected ones from reviews of my contributions made to a poetry website. The effort of compiling and publishing this work is aimed at sharing my feelings about everyday events with poetry lovers around the globe.

Dedication

First and foremost, I want to thank and praise the Almighty God for His special gift of words that has made this compilation of my poems a reality. By the grace of God, together with perseverance and the peace of mind, I am grateful that I can now contribute and share my work with other poetry enthusiasts all over the world.

My special dedication goes to my beloved mum, Haw Tek Neo, my spouse, Chong Kwee Yau and my three lovely children—Alex Wee Lik Yang, Daphne Wee Lik Wei and Nicholas Wee Lik Ken for being my inspiration.

Next, I would like to dedicate this compendium of poems to all my siblings—Gary Wee Kok Wah, Michael Wee Kok Tai, Dr. Jennifer Wee Beng Neo, Peter Wee Kok Cheng and Henry Wee Kok Leng, who have been instrumental in my growing up years. My dedication also goes to all my nephews, nieces and in-laws.

Finally, my sincere thoughts go to my late father, Wee Eng Kim and sister, Wee Kwee Neo for their relentless support.

Adrian Wee Kok Seng

Epigraph

The voice of a poet is synonymous to the reality of life in action

&

If only the blind could lead the way, those with sight should be
more able to walk with confident strides

[1] A bad choice?

Do I have a choice to say things I don't wish to?
I do when I'm determined it'll never be from me
It'll be all about me
My dignity will be at stake
I'll not gamble my life for it
I'm not a loser to admit defeat
I'm not at fault, even if I decline it
I have my reservations, my principles
Stay close and be respectful, please
Just to stay relevant and respected as always

Do I have a choice to say things I don't wish to?
I don't when I wish for transparency
A wish is only a wish
What's a wish anyway?
A dead dream, not even a syllogism
Logical thinking if there is
A bad dream to expect ready to reveal
A man's logic is still dead in sin
Overtaken most by ill-feelings, alive in the blood
Dead to the foreskin and guilty eyes
Only the time will come and arrest
Just like Ananias and Sapphira
The blunder cost them their lives
All for the bad reason, a bad choice

Keep the eyes and ears open
There'll be times of lingered testing
The moment the wrong step sets in
The buzzer of pain sounds the game
A trying moment it will be
All because of wrong pleasures set in mind
Pleasing to the ears but blind eyes will cause the fall
A painful fall, besieged by convenient handshakes
The downfall of morale, the beginning of misery
Stop it and get away
While grace still abounds

[2] A bad dream

Down by the creek
I saw myself rowing
The oars don't seem to be working
Funny dreams, keeping me stunned
Against the current, even still air is ruling
What am I doing, down the creek?
My soul is lifted up and away

Down the creek again
Driven by the conversations
Mundane but now, it's taking me away
To a place I don't think I rightfully belong
A far place in the unknown
I can't be sure
I am not sure

This can't be real
It's only a nasty dream
Away with it
Let me go, let me go
Whew, I'm back.
My soul is back
I'll never have that conversation again!

[3] A confession

I know who I am
I keep no enmity with men
I know I just can't retaliate
Angered, I will not revenge

I know who I am
I may be mortal weak
My predicaments may leave me upset
I've found myself renewed sublimed

I know who I am
I will not let small concerns overtake me
I'm strong in my weakness
I'm a victor in my afflictions

[4] A special day

Another beautiful day
A creative and well-crafted reminder
The faithfulness of the Creator
Lighting the universe
Over both the strong and the weak
Over the wealthy and the needy
The rainbow may not appear
But the light says it all

Today, the first of the new year
Celebrations are everywhere
Nations of all tongues
People from all walks of life
Together they make exuberant noise
Rejoicing and merry-making, past midnight
Leaving the meaningful and ugly past behind
Marching forward in gleeful decorations

Let's make the day
Purposeful and meaningful it will be
Not just today but the days after
Bringing hopes to the hopefuls
Bringing cheer to the downcast
Bringing smiles to the forgotten
Melting grieving hearts away

[5] A wonderful make

Why feel easily offended?
We are all the same
Smart, creative, annoying
They are part of the human traits
Forget not,
We are one too
Just that nobody told us so

Call me lovely
You have provided for others too
Be glad, you are a package
A beautifully delivered package
Sent not by the mailman
Rather, you are a special delivery
Strong, bold, loving and kind

Be not pessimistic
Rather be optimistic
You are a special make
Brand new, everyday
Nice compliments, great thoughts
Critics, take no offence
Scolding, don't take it personal

Positive and negative, they are one
To make us wholesome and desired
We are special

[6] Amazing love

Who can ever tell when I'm happy or sad?
Only those who understand will say I do
True confession and feelings of the experienced
None can ever deny, albeit it's for real

Reality is often the face to face struggle
When I am sad, I must not look sad
Lest people will say I want to be sympathized
When I am happy, I must not feel overwhelmed
Lest people will say that's not my usual self
What else can I do when I'm always noticed?

My presence is representative of kind words and deeds
One who seems to understand everything
Everything under the sky
My joy is secretly hidden in my pain
The unexpected growth in the body is not my game

However, I can testify the goodness of my God
He knows what's best for me and my family
I can now rest assure He's good
Even in my doubt, He dwells nearby
Everyone around seems a blessing now

What else can I ask
If not for His saving grace?
Broken and confused I've been
Now I can confidently say, He's by my side
My comfort and my redeemer

Of all the distress I have
He has set the way
I will not turn back ever
Turning back would mean more misery
A journey nobody will be drawn to
An experience of seeing pain and distress

I am convinced now
This is all I have
And all that I have is a gift
A special gift
Never to neglect
Taken for granted will not be my way
Now and forever more, I'll surely trust Him

[7] An ugly past

The sea of water in the valley
Left me a thought
If I crossed it, I'd be a river of no return
If I didn't cross it, I'll be called

I'd just ask my superior
"Would you do it if you were me?"
Adamant and stubborn lines would cloud his mind
A punishment it turned out to be

You should have come earlier
I did, blame nature for it
I could only do what I could
The rest it was all destined

The defense,
None can ever comment
I escaped

[8] Availability matters

My presence matters
My limbs to share the chores
Let my beloved do it alone
Never will I let it happen

The lady's expectation is beyond imagination
Be there and make the self at hand
Papers may be read later and together
Tired minds now energized, love overrules

The presence rekindles genuine vows
The sanctity once pledged, witnessed by all
The touch of love indescribable, so eminent
My way to illustrate I care after my declaration
"I do"

[9] Be real

It gets closer by the minute
Why worry? I'm still breathing
Oh yea, feeling very sure?
No assurance, no words of comfort

When it comes knocking at the door
No eyes can deny and deceive it
Only the body is present
The soul is now absent

Cries and hugs of agony fill the air
Mourning for a lost beloved
Tears of mixed reactions cover conversations
Look, it's for real
Are we ready?

It comes like the wind
You can feel it and not run from it
It comes as gentle shadows
Moving to the rear
Suddenly disappear

[10] Be thankful

The little things we have
More precious than anything valued
Should we complain?

The child we raise
We are fully entrusted

The love we shower
Its worth is deeper than the sea

The shelter we provide
The least we can afford

The home we create
The priceless gift of all

The food we serve
The overflowing blessing that will remain

For as long as we know
And for as long as we appreciate
We will be thankful
All the days of our lives

Rise above all occasions
See the light at the tunnel's end
There is always hope
Even when there seems none

Reign strong over sight
That's faith
It is simply because
We are thankful

[11] Beauty in display

Look at the open sky after twilight
The numerous stars, symbolical of the infinite promises
Many will come to pass
Only if we know how to get them fulfilled

How I wish I can be a star
Not a movie star
But a twinkling star
A star that brightens the dark firmament
And speaks life to the gazer

Gaze at it and you'll see
An unusual discovery
One that reveals life's measure
The star is like the many scenes
Displaying the innovative creation of life there is

The many scenes the star will distinctively display
Scenes of love across the meadow
Beauty of the deep blue ocean too
A memory of the great lovely past
One which will now duplicate
A promising life beyond

Incomparable beauty
Though mystical
Lovely to gaze
Forever it will be
A symbol of might
A symbol of unwavered hope

But most of all
Its beauty in display

[12] Care to share

Care to part
Everything you have
Others will be glad
Yours a gift of life
Pledge and you'll be blessed

Nobody knows what comes next
Shout and make known
Given life is life passed on
Anxious, scared?
No reason to be one

What's left is best given
A life given is heaven sent moment

[13] Celebrate

Shout your heart out
Make everyone around amaze
Make it known
Declare it!

There is joy in sadness
There is hope in disappointment
There is peace in distress
There is strength in hunger
There are blessings at play

Life's a game
A discovery
That makes or breaks us
To pieces we'll never be

Rise to the occasion
Above all situations
Victors we are
A proclamation so strong and true
Amazing truth

There's no turning back
No backstabbing
No curse words
Only words of kindness
That will sustain and remain
Till the last breath is breathed

Knowing that all is going to be fine
Only if I know how to and do it right
Dealing with situations my best

[14] Celebrations

Celebrations come and go
Many types and moods shared
All leading to one ultimate reason
A time to share and be joyful
At least it is celebrated again

Celebrations bring lots of untold changes too
What a reunion and a time of togetherness
Months passed by, probably years
Now the special occasion of the year
Even Valentine's Day may not substitute

Friends drop by to say Hi!
Exchanges of greetings and words
Encouragements amid the free flow of conversations
Truly, hearts are again bonded and made closer
An understanding to a better world of communication

[15] Check it out!

Be wary always
Everything can be uncertain
Nothing gets delivered for free
Without purpose, so to speak

Believe not it's meant for me
Sure about it?
Celebrations may turn into mourning
Many have fallen
All because of simplicity

A great price to pay indeed
It's not funny
I'm not exaggerating
I was once a victim
Lost my pride and confidence

I've learnt not to be enticed
Life can take an ugly turn
The bends can be life-threatening
Diminishing all prospects
Trust, innocence, agility

Put an end to it
There'll be more coming
Stay vigilant and careful
Secrets to a saving grace

[16] Complaints

In abundance
We call it a blessing

In need
We complain we are deprived

In pain
We complain "It's not fair"

In joy
We say "It's time"

In sorrow
We complain "why at this time?"

In goodness
We say "We deserve it"

In creation
We say "It's God's will"

In love
We say "We're meant to be together"

In divorce
We say "There's no compromise"

In short
We have to learn to accept

[17] Confession

Know that you are special
Because you are born special
Special in your own way
Special in the way you think
Special in the way you do things
Special in your careful choice of words
Your special trademark

Know that you are unique
Unique in your personal speech
Unique in how you treat others
Unique in how you walk your talk
Unique in all your dealings
Your unique self-presentation

Know that you are lovely
Lovely in your ways
The way you express your thoughts
The way your thoughts reach the hundreds
The way your loveliness grow into passion
The passion to serve with no reservations
The ever loving kindness that grows and blooms

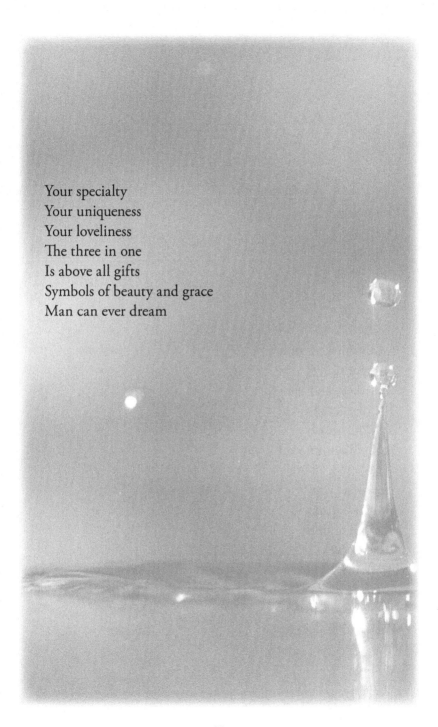

Your specialty
Your uniqueness
Your loveliness
The three in one
Is above all gifts
Symbols of beauty and grace
Man can ever dream

[18] Creation at stake

Life is a God-given promise
A blessing
A wonder
A miracle
Appreciate it
Love it
Protect it

A commitment in hand
A responsibility
To protect and uphold
The dignity of man
And the breath
From His Immortal Being

Stop destroying
Stop polluting
The call of duty
To preserve
Be clear
Green is life
The gift of Nature
For man's kindred

No more destruction
Let us save the remainder
Remember our children
And their children's generation
Life is something
Keep it, preserve it
Our survival is at stake

[19] Cruise along

The journey I take
Daily, down the streets of gold
Exciting returns at the end of the day
After all, I am called to serve and be grateful

I am cruising along the river that promises no returns
I am satisfied, contented of what I do
Silver or gold is not my goal
After all, this borrowed life is temporarily sure

The journey I take
It will come to a complete cycle
A cycle with a satisfied declaration
I've done my best, let me now rest myself to restore

[20] Dare say it?

I've never lied, believe me
Who will if each time we speak
Blunders and hurts fill the air?
Hearts are made to turn away
Overcome by rambling gossips
Only the sober will pacify the self
It's ok, he's only a man

I've never been sincere, believe me
Who will now, that man is like a shadow
Not a real thing to claim but only a representation
Sincerity would boast not the superiority of the self
Rather, it's often misjudged and misinterpreted
Only the beholder of the self can testify of it—no defense

I've never regretted my doings, believe me
Even if I do, it's done and I can't change it
Shakespeare's what's done can't be undone stays
Get real and reel on to doing it right
That's the expectation of a simple mind
Just accept it, move on, none will do it for you

[21] Delays

Take five becomes take ten
A living curse that will live on
Difficult to change
Difficult to kill
Only in due course
Unbelieving shame changing its course

An undying habit
Too good to bid goodbye
An unwelcomed shame
Only chains of love will break
Destiny may hold strong
The waves of change bringing new hope

Total recall binds the soul
Get rid of it and soar above
Get over it and deliver the self
Catastrophes and calamities
Modern day tragedies so destructive
A time to pray and not to stray

[22] Designed to raise

You are one in a million
A rare gem
Possessing remarkable traits
Love, patience, kindness, longsuffering
True gifts that are envied
To help wean and raise
The little charges, put under your care

In a vast, uncertain world
A flag-bearer you have been
A provider, a friend and a fine example
Leading your innocent, young offspring
Naive of circumstances
Exceptionally, a disciplinarian too
Sparing not the rod of correction
When situations warrant it
Well-being has always been
Your utmost concern
For all the best possible life's gains

Only God knows the pains you bear
The life you've pledged to live
The hope of a future you wish to see in us
Rightfully, every single thing has been predestined
None can ever comprehend what's in store
Until bliss or grief openly reveals
The victory or defeat to mean circumstances
But you had maintained your peace, feeling assured
Knowing trials and temptations are just but
A camouflage that fervently matures us, over time

Your pure sacrifices of tireless routines
The undeterred smiles on your tired face say it all
Your motto, "Count it all joy in the days of trouble"
Mind-boggling yet inspirational indeed

[23] Different but special

Ladies' cool
Image of femininity
Guys' build
Strength declared
Revealed and unsung

Provoke not
Make peace
Mutual image and strength
The binding force
Together we'll stand

[24] Don't go astray

Don't cheat life for a day
It will come haunting all day
Probably months and years to stay
Recognize the blasphemy it brings
More misery than life can contain

Take it easy each day
The next day can be hay in daylight
Another day can be life swayed to the cliff's edge
Get settled with what is in hand
Dream not for more as it's greed in play

A game many gave in so easily
Death is at the end, waiting and wondering
If more can be game for it
A battle nobody usually wins
Instead, great losses and pains reign in the veins

Wanting more but there's a limit
A reminder
Don't be one
It's cursed to the toes
Endless headaches and heartaches
Will continue to be shame in store

Only we can decide and choose
The only way out
Not to pursue further but abstain

[25] Don't tell me

Don't tell me
That I'm ugly
It hurts
Beyond my pride

Don't tell me
That I'm beautiful
It's like walking on cloud nine
Like the peacock's stretched, colorful tail feathers

Don't tell me
That I'm hardworking
It makes everyone envious
Only to be slayed by the shrew

Don't tell me
That I'm sensitive
Who isn't so?
Only the response will make a show

Don't tell me
That I should stop blaming
I can live being cursed and shamed
My dignity is at stake

Don't tell me
I should do it
Everybody does it innocently
I can't be guilty because of poor judgment

Don't tell me
I should just move away
Who dares command me so?
My life has always been a liberty

Don't tell me
That I shouldn't reciprocate
I'm born with the love to share
Get along with me

[26] Down memory lane

The day I first cried
As I was delivered
I became part of the bargain
A gift of hope to mum and dad

The day I started babbling
Untold joys on their faces
My child is talking
He's alright after all

The day I brought life to the family
The school grades seem so wonderful
A genius to rule the future is here
A trust fund is in the file

The day I graduated
New hope sparked in the eyes
My duty is done
God bless his journey down the crooked roads

The day I got married
Everyone was full of expectation
Anticipating cheerful and comforting words
Delivered as I walked down the aisle

I am free now
Not really, my obligation begins
A parent I will now be
Expecting a new arrival, I once was

[27] End of the year again

Resolutions now up for a check
Listed promises fulfilled?
Strayed life an improved change?
Every reason now a commitment?
See it not again
List it not another routine
Cliché-talk—the die-hard habit

Rise and live above them
Mean it and get them delivered
An achievement, not to boast
An accomplishment, not to silent the world
An achiever's right to once again
Set untold promises, only to prove his worth
The end will see it realized
A victory that will never die

Face it and live by its standards
Delivering success stories
Not to self-praise
Not to take the honor
Only to declare
I believe I can
I know I can
The secret success
To a new year's beginning

[28] Every day judgment

What can I say
When I am judged all the way?

I am called a liar when I tell the truth
I am called cruel when what I mean is well
I am called a cheat when I try to salvage my rights
I am called stupid when my conscience is clear
I am called a warrior when all voices are drowned by fear
I am called brutal when my life is at threat
I am called a success when everyone else suffer from defeat
I am called a wonder when what I did is truly beyond
    imagination

Being positive is being a winner
Being negative is being naive and a loser
Whatever I am called
I can't deceive myself
When what I mean is well after all
A manifestation of the self
My beliefs
My life

[29] Everything's great

Look back and ponder again
The many good things that have happened
But why are we still complaining?

If we think we are poor,
There are many more who are in want

If we think we have not been fairly treated
Who has ever claimed that they have been fairly treated?

If we think we have not been given the opportunity
How many opportunities would you consider enough?

If we think we have not been given the education we deserve
How many have been contented feeling they have received
enough?

At least, we are not poor
Enough to keep us from being hungry

At least, we have the opportunities
Enough to say we have been given the chance

We have some basic education
Enough to fend for ourselves

There are many more things we may ask
Look again
Everywhere across the globe
People are suffering
Not a choice for them
But circumstances have made them so
Not their asking
But they have become the footstool
Of the ravens and vultures
Advocating no mercy but suppression

Depression takes center stage
More cries of uncalled suffering
Only the end of breath will silence their cries
Until the suppressors realize
It's their doing and repent
To the benefit of humankind

[30] Flow along

Keep me company
In my journey
To a land of the hopefuls
Promises of good returns
Not dreamers' dreams
For dreams do come through

Keep me company
In my journey
To the land of milk and honey
Promises of joy and happiness
Joining hands in love and liberty
Delivering hungry souls looking for directions

Keep me company
In my journey
To the land of wealth and health
Promises that keep me going
Knowing I'm witnessing it
From the day I gave my life believing it

[31] Food for thought

If Albert Camus strongly opines
Not to walk behind me
Cos' I will not lead
And not to walk in front of me
Cos' I will not follow
But walk beside me
And be my friend
Suggests life's mistaken concepts
Lead on

Often, we follow but we don't follow through
Often, we lead but we turned dismay
Rather, walk hand in hand
To a blooming friendship
Surpassing regrets
Overcoming differences
The only known similarity
We are all leaders
Born to lead just the same

Over the years, wisdom will set in
Revealing man's only flaw
Only time and tide will lead on
Waiting for none to shine

[32] Get in tune

Get in tune
Against the world's melodious sounds
Pleasant listening on the outside but deep inside
It's all about the self and selfish wants
Believe and dance not in its tune
It's all shadows of what's to come

Everyone's tune may not be our tune
We differ so much in almost everything
Everything seems so genuine
Keep refining and stay tuned
The just shall know and be free
The wise shall be warriors in life
The simple shall be models of victory

Get in tune
Find the direction
A direction where genuine promises abide
That all may live and dwell well
In a land filled with promises of life abundant
Till the end wraps its arms around all

A mistaken tune has overtaken many
Crippling souls of all ages and wisdom
Only those tuned in will say, "I survive"
Thank God I'm saved
I'll now march on

[33] Getting it right

The start can be the most painful
Trying to help out with the chores
Driving in the stormy weather with very little choice left
Rushing through the paper work, messing every step
Listening to constant naggings and unfeeling souls

But, ponder again
It is our time and season
A payback clockwork when we could have realized
Everything is a cycle, not too vicious I suppose

Hold it close and remain composed
Reflect as that's the ultimate best we can do
Pacifying the self, it's now mine
To grow and learn patience in every circumstance

Mature we will be, the more pains the better
All because complaints do no good than bring hurtful
    feelings
Say "It's okay"
I'll bear with it

Chain the probing thoughts, see the liberty
You'll soon grow to appreciate
As they have always been

[34] Gift revealed

Be bold
Be strong
You are one in a million
You will discover your gift
A gift not to be missed

Use it
Encourage seeking souls
Drowned in sorrows
Unfounded but real
Care to say
Appreciate it
You can do it
I believe strongly

Now, do it
Step forward
Claim it
You'll know it
The best discovery
Revealed in your time

[35] Give in not

The best I have put in
Suddenly cripples my inner being
Have I been sidelined and forgotten?
Have I been taken for granted?
A journey so unfair to me
But's what's fair?
Should I continue to please others?

I have my life to live
I have my health to care for
I have a career that is so dear
I have my obligation to render
I have my friends to cheer
I have everything except for the confusion
I feel lost and confused

Worth to sacrifice so well and yet go unnoticed?
Am I a victim of convenience
Or am I not up to the mark?
Marked and marked down
The onset to destroy all that is laid
I'm not challenged
I know things will change
Because I'm changing even if the expected is not imminent

I'm beginning to learn to accept
My failure in one is not the end of my sacrifices
I'll persist till the game is fairly played
Relationships will be strongly mended again
All for a good cause
After all the honest and sincere battles
Of reliving the glorious past
And maintaining, all for a noble cause

[36] Go slow

Lift your head high with care
Lest you'll experience a painful fall unaware

Regret the ugly past now and not later
Or more regrets will come haunting for sure

Create an achievable goal for yourself
As good goals are not to be put on the shelf

Praise not thyself and celebrate, thinking it's your day
Rather, commend life-breathing moments
And watch every word you say

Declare courageously the affirmative
Cease highlighting the negative

Boats and ships may sail and sink without trace
But we can always learn to fend and keep our face

The words of life can do wonders
But keep them simple and meaningful first

[37] Gratitude

Why complain?
Many do not even have it
A complete, normal physical gift
No visible disabilities,
No basic needs lacking

Everything's a package,
So perfectly endowed
Our possession are our blessings
Our lacking is not to lament
Complain not to feel wanting

Share the blessings
Keeping them restraints the flow
Sharing them overflows all
Make the difference
Complain no more

Acts of justice prevail much more
Overflowed with unknowing gifts
Initiate the move and see streams of hopes
Channels of life-giving opportunities untold
Unwrapping possibilities of life, hope and bliss

[38] Hear the call

Calls in many forms come our way
Calls for help out of desperation
Calls for commitment in solemnization
Calls for trust as the anchor of a long-lasting bond

A mother's call for help is indeed worth complementing
A sibling's call for help is worth considering
Their calls for help are worth pondering
When else can a saint learn obedience?

Nature's call is not to be ignored either
Ignorance will bleed with suffering
Contain not what should not remain
The cycle is great, a moment of liberty

[39] Hold on

Hold on
You will make it
Believe me

I was there before
Thinking!
Hoping very earnestly

My hero, my savior
Rescued me
Out of the ditch

I found my exit
Rescued and delivered
Am satisfied now

A teacher I will be
Comforting, showing the way
To liberty, safety

[40] I am blessed

Blessed, we are called
Raised with utmost passion
Elder siblings' help is sure
Younger ones come for comforting words

Friends say we are indispensable
Teachers say we are okay
What do you say?

Play safe now
Never be easily duped
Words conveyed are life and death

Simply interpreted is danger
Moderate interpretation is safer
Just interpretation is life-protected

Whatever people may say
You can safely say
I am convinced
Nothing can ever overtake me
Unless it's granted

I am protected
By grace I'll continue
Knowing I am in safe hands
All the way

[41] I am uniquely special

Am I lying
If I say I'm happy?
Am I telling the truth
When I say I miss you?
Am I pulling your legs
When I whisper words of love out of nowhere?

Believe me if you will
I mean it well
I know what I'm doing and saying
These are the colors of life
That paint every brook and stream
The true image of me
My trait and identity

I love surprising people
As I love surprises
They can harm me not
I'm cautious, I know
Words are not expressed without feelings
Actions are not shown without thoughts
Words and actions are harmoniously paired
Meant well only from a heart that yells

You'll be fine
You can trust me

[42] I discovered myself

Dawn has yet to declare its rule
The anxious wait of a mother
Thrilled with the coming of her newborn
In pain, she waited
The moment nearing 4 a.m. came
Blessed with a prince

The joy on her face
A thousand words cannot recall
In the dimly-lit room
Tears of joy silenced cricket sounds
A future as a company
Not a serendipity
The time has come, revealed

A companion in old age
True it has been
Here I am, encouraging
Doing my duty when there's none
I'm glad it's done
My love, my life
My sacrifice, a little light
In return for the tired nights

Buying each chime as time glides
Nothing compared to the patience
Sighted later as fond memories glow
Cheers of resounding praise
None can ever forget
Neither will we ever be
Ungrateful, blaming the difficult years

Behold the sanctity of life
Pure and white, ruling over pains and strife
I've discovered it right
Before my very eyes
Pleasing and celebrating my giving back

[43] I may be

I may be down
But I am not troubled
I may be tired
But I will stay vigilant

I may be accused
But I will hold my fort
I may be despised
But I will continue to rise

I may be scolded
But I know I'm doing it right
I may be admired
But it's not worth feeling great

I may be a rising poet
But my talent is His to honor
I may be praised
But I can only say I'm only a vessel

I may be good-looking
But good looks are just a temporary sketch
And I may be cautious
All because I've learnt

My experiences, my teacher
Not exchangeable
My treasured memoir

[44] I recall

The morning journey down the road
Impatience overtook me
I steered and given room to navigate
Thanks to conscience-clear motorists

Out of traffic, I safely veered
Whew! Am grateful
Now, on my way

Half a day's meeting and training
Overshot and detoured
Right to the doorstep
Welcomed to start

A day of words exchanged
Ideas and opinions so massive
Hovering across the room
Fine exchanges of discourse

Enquiries filled the air
Familiar faces around
Informally connected
Now a friend till the next gathering

Lovely, splendid moments
Laughter and jokes filled the air
Tickled but not pickled
All to remain and stay germaine

[45] I will be

An accomplished poet I will be
Brought around with gifts untold
Discovering the beauty of life
Expressed in words and feelings unfold

Great words, backing the vigilant strides
Overtaking life in motivating tones
Bring life, bring hope to seeking hearts and souls
Upright they'll be and grace they'll humbly see

I will not let life be clamped to vanity
Break every chain of ugly binds
There will be relief, there will be harmony
The hope to love and share with the might of the pen

I may not know of tomorrow
But it will surely knock on my door
I will not turn around and just go
For I know what I can do and I will do it all

[46] I'll regret not

This morning you were so sunny
Then, suddenly the downpour
Even now, everything's gone into the ground
Drained and wasted fifty of mine
From the sweat of the person I just paid
Now, I can only sigh in despair
Thanksgiving is closing in

Hey, hey, that's okay
Not everything will be taken away
Even if it will be far from sight, face it
It's a reality
Nobody can ever understand it
At least I had the opportunity
To get it done my best
Just unfortunately, the rain reigned

If that can blatantly happen
Incensed not for what right have we to complain
Everything happens with an explanation
A reason only the enquirer understands
Hopefully so, otherwise it's time to restore
Keep ugliness at bay and away
While closing in to beauty, the gateway to a hearty day
Turning unpleasant notions into dancing

[47] If only I could

If only I could
I would want to relive my childhood days
Paddling on the brown and lightweight palm fruit
Fishing out puffer fish and seeing them jump on the sand
Playing with the catapult, shooting tiny fruit, making the
    body itch
Blocking the tiny streams for some mysterious catfish
Lighting up the harmless-looking "fireworks" and gaily
    shout for joy

If only I could
I would want to turn the clock back
Seeing myself talking and helping the needy
Understanding their agony and hatred for life
Cheering them with the best words of encouragement I know
Renewing their hope, climbing the winding pathways
Growing strengths anew and making hopes glow
Lest defeat takes precedence, failing every effort

If only I could
I would want to lay a dozen roses to welcome her home
Making her feel special and know she is a gift from above
Loved and cared for with no conditions attached
Spoiling her with fine dining treats and hospitality
Building a character, cherished forever and adorable for life

[48] Just being positive

I am seeking
All that is possible
Looking into all possibilities
That I am not only a believer
I will pursue whatever it takes
Cos' I am a firm believer of justice

The justice to enjoy my rights
Superiors will call it a privilege
To me, justice served is justice deserved
Whatever it may cost
No noble cause will go unheeded
There will be rebels of the same cause

What I seek is what I firmly believe
It will come to pass
A surprise it will be
In the appropriate time as destined
It will be revealed and made known
A stupendous revelation it will be

Changed lives is what I see
Lifted hearts is what I feel
Joyful souls is what I notice
The spread of hope
Akin to the melting snow
Gliding the mountain slopes
That's dunames
My accomplished plea

[49] Just me

Everyone's calling
For a share of work
A distribution of a "fair share"
A workload nobody cares

Pretty faces seem a nightmare
Beautiful inside, can I share?
Who can ever bear that?
True souls will not want to compare

Why share?
Isn't this your share?
The wrong choices
The mistaken personality

The wayward inroads
The blatant words
Pick up your armor
Stay cool and mystical

It's divine wisdom
Called to subdue the mind
Even if it's unfair
Take the stride with prayer

I'm not to take the glory
It isn't mine to keep
It's a mission entrusted
Shine and reach out

Settle for a change
An understanding of the simple hearted
Worth more than diamonds
And gold compared

To the return of creation
Simple conversations
Simple communion
Simple rest in the garden
The garden in creation

[50] Justified

Send me words of comfort
You'll be adored, appreciated

Send me a bouquet of flowers
I'll call you romantic

Send me a surprise
I'll carve it in memory all my life

Send me help
I'll treasure it much

Send me a sincere notion
I'll be thinking, your intention

Send me for a chore
I'll do it with my all

Send me a companion
I'll walk with her wherever she goes

Send me a structure
I'll complete it to my best

Send me a broken heart
I'll mend, restore it again

Send me a lost child
I'll make sure she gets home comforted

Send me a critic
I'll reflect on it

Send me a warning
I'll learn from it and be better later

Send me a hope
I'll send just the same to another

Finally send me a note
I'll frame it to glow in my dim shadow

[51] Justified truth

Educated or uneducated
Industrious or lazy
Rich or poor
Thin or fat
Conditions one chooses to be

Immature beginning
Set to march on
A realization later
Calling for a change
A change for the better

Praised and complimented all the way
A new image in the horizon
All for acceptance sake
Admired traits and expectations
All but a camouflage of life and vanity

Be contented and grateful
We are what and who we are
Change comes with readiness
Acceptance is then the result
The newness of life and hope treading on

[52] Keep me up

Umpteen times we fell
Nobody was there to pull us up
Probably, everyone's so busy
Bogged down by all the cares of the world
Really, the feeling of being neglected and rejected
Is not a pleasant story to tell
Let alone, our so-called friends
Are they real and true to really care?

To ask how we are
How we feel
How we cope with it
Hopes are now dashed
The trust is now proven vain
Their true colors have really surfaced
Truths that seem hard to swallow
Can we complain?

Even if we can, will the pain be gone?
The moment of truth has finally come
That's a fact that will continue
Haunting us in bad dreams

Wake up
We need not remain but rise
Rise above the storm and raging waves
The survival we keep as a conquest
Until we learn and really come to our senses
Just to keep us marching
For as long as time ticks away

[53] Keep rolling

Say Hello!
Everybody's so busy
Never mind
Keep moving

Stay focused
You'll notice
There will be response
Hi, Hello!
A return note

That's today's society
Taken in by all flavors
Mystical as it may sound
Stay strong to prolong
Lest you be just like everybody
Lonely and misty
Cheering others

[54] Keep strolling

I hear and I forget
True for a learner,
Forced to remember
But overtaken by failures

I see and I remember
More truth is seen
Opportunity, the catalyst of learning

I do and I understand
The antidote to acquiring
The effervescence of life's lessons

A journey of a thousand miles
Can begin with a single step
A new approach, a new hope
For the valiant and the strong in heart

What if it fails?
It doesn't really matter
Just pick yourself up and walk again
A cycle it can be
But the end matters most

Press on and walk, if you cannot run
You'll come to the finishing line
Your stride, your hope, your achievement
At last it will be

That's only the beginning.
Keep strolling

[55] Let them grow

Children are children
Forever they'll think like one
A time to play their favorite game
What else . . . computer games
A time to watch their favorite channel
What else . . . cartoons interpolated with violence
That's what children's life is

Will we ever let that destruction reign?
The seemingly entertaining
While destroying morale built over time
Or would we stop the clock and rebuild
The lost time is not the lost opportunity to remodel

Children are children
They can be shaped into wonders
Love shapes their hearts
Care shapes their attitudes
Patience shapes their character
Kindness shapes their well-being
Most of all, a person is shaped to live
Victoriously above all influence and threats

Give them the life they deserve
They will in turn provide us
The life we so desire
If not in the present
They will be mindful
Our old age, they'll be
There and always for us

[56] Life's a great lesson

Life, to many, is a bore
To some, life is a symbol of freedom
Freedom to engage in crazy dreams
Unknown of its destiny

Be wary though of life's promises
Beautiful they may seem but be not deceived
Sweet things may appear appealing and lovely
The truth is often a reverse, a disaster regrettable

Be quick however, to ponder but be slow to act
The thoughts of man are seemingly wisdom limited
Desire and seek His wisdom—His ways, His thoughts
Your path to a goal-directed and real life liberty

Rejoice therefore, life is after all a puzzle
Solutions so amazingly crafted, beautifully designed
Reach out and you'll be dumbfounded
By His amazing, unfailing grace ever

[57] Life's a treat

The birds are back
Singing gleefully
Breaking the silence of dawn
The rising sun quietly sits in the horizon
Gazed and admired
Beautiful as ever

The rain is no exception
Another form of divine infusion
Life for the farmers
Rain or shine
Both are seasonably anticipated
Time to get on and make the bucks
To lay out the expected meal
All after a hard day's work

The display of nature's gift
Amazing grace that will not phase out
Tones of gladness and cheerful shouts
Making every minute a celebration
Life for the children especially
Simple and pleasurable life
Is all they seek
That's it
Life's a treat

[58] Life's like a wish

Life is like a poet
Writing his gift of love
A gift that certainly impacts
Creating waves of summer
Melting snow on mountain tops
Diminishing dew when morning calls
Embracing newness of hope magnified

Life is like music
Singing its melody in joyful steps
Synchronizing sounds after drum beats
Creating heartfelt gratitude for life extended
Developing streaks of entertaining colors
Moving the simple hearts to seek peace afar

Ultimately, life's like a stream
Caressing each side of the river bed
The creepers alongside suddenly become alive
The river of life springs forth unexpected motions
Creating satiable moods that seem to last forever
All for the beauty as nature calls and provides

[59] Listen

Be strong for it is your character
Be upright for it protects your reputation
Be wise for it saves you all the trouble
Be watchful for it gives you security

Character is like a shadow that rises and falls
Men's greed can change it all
From a beautiful rainbow to a destructive storm
What's left is nothing but it's all because of a bad cause

Uprightness has been a bad game played
Integrity is no longer a must to hold and behold
Lost honor is unimaginably ghostly once foretold
Virtue is to be virtually upheld against all rolling threats

Wisdom on the other hand is divine presence
Ticking away destructive intentions, chaos is set afar
Grow in it and be blessed throughout the age
Its worth's more than knowledge abound and riches untold

Vigilance bears security, the worry of safety
Building walls of confidence, breaking all odds
Reminding perpetrators they are being watched
We are alert and we know what's best for us

[60] Love strikes the note

The moment I set my brown eyes on you
I was way ready to settle for a deal
A promise I'll make to myself and to my God
To consider myself fortunate to meet my missing self

The complement was stupendous
Marvelous as the morning dew
The cool of the morning air
Struck a note that will remain a life opportunity

The pumping of the heart was unbelievably abnormal
It's love at first sight
Wedding bells rang soon after
The bond was beyond description

Life took a turn and change for the better
Singlehood, now a duty to hold and behold
Despite all rumors and calamities
I'll be by your side

I know I'll be loved too
Mutual love we will share
That's meant for us
To keep and protect
Till we are apart
Not by choice but when it's time

So, cling to it
We'll be fine
Forever it will be
As we submit to each other
Till the day is done

[61] Manners

If I say I have manners
I will show it in our conversations
A conversation that will strike a note
Revealing the beauty secrets of the person I am

If I say I am filial
I will illustrate my filial-piety
A clear sign of my sincerity and infallible equity
Creating waves that will speak volumes of your pride

If I say I have your attributes in me
The things I do will reflect much of you
Your pride of me will I keep close to my heart
And I'll lift your integrity, your pride, till I fall

[62] Maturing lessons

Events are surprises
Uplifting they can be
Destruction they may bring
Arresting hearts to the ground

Learning comes with them
Lessons not immediately realized
They are but part of a journey
A preparation
To more complicated ones

Run not
Face the fact
Life's not easily taken
Damage may be done
But we will be preserved

Believe it
We are all destined
Not to perish
Not a wish
Till the day is done

[63] My new companion

Purchase with conditions
Interest free for 12 months
Amazing apps and newness of life
An exploration that's worth an investment for life

Slim and feather weight it is
Cleared over 12 staggered payments
A pain by the month I'll endure
Gladness will soon surface by year-end after all

Plenty to discover and learn
My work stored and restored
Technology has great wonders
My work is done in seconds

A great wonder
A wonderful help
My aid and friend
My wonderful companion in store

[64] Mysteries

Life, to many, is a mystery
Mysterious in many ways
Mysterious in many forms
Friends turning their backs on us
Colleagues calling us power crazy
Superiors denying our simple rights
They call rights privileges

What's happening?
Have they not learnt?
Have they forgotten?
Life's truly a mystery
Conceived out of pride
Overruled by misjudgments
Rule over the controlled imaginations
Concealed mysteries subdued finally

Dwell not in mysteries
Trouble not the self
They are a mind game
Probing the conscience
The intellectuals lose their logic
Drowned by unrefined syllogism
Failure to grasp is not fatal
Only persistent courage counts them all
Mysteries may influence the carnal mind
Start to wonder,
Enigmatic and Dumbfounded we become

Reason now and take the center stage
Be not alarmed
Be not perplexed
They are messages to disclose
Navigating the undecorated window
Baring life as it should be
Seen and wondered

[65] Mystical

Every desire and need
Every dream and pursuit
Every worry and anxiety
Spices of discoveries
Noble keys to unlocking mysteries

Fret not
It's kind of maturing lessons
A lesson too slow to learn for many
Yet every happening is a blessing concealed
Only the wise is awestruck and quick to acquire

Think not yonder
They may come like flood waters
Trying to diminish our existence
An existence so dear to trade
Hold the fort and witness the sight

Rounds of defining lessons
Seemingly dark shades that will turn bright
Stay watchful and doubt not
Stay above the drowning waters
You'll see the light, life and hope
The existence of all meaningful creations

[66] Name-calling

Labels are common
Labeling people with different words
Positive, negative labels

A trend is shaped
An identification
For easier calling

Calling people names
A disrespect?
Sieve it and offend not

As much as we dislike another
It stinks, also a displeasure
An identity we carry
Our entire life, a burden

Balding and now greying all over
Smart but now unemployed
Good-looking but still looking and eligible
Fast but a loser on track

A norm to identify others
A significant loss of identity
Now, all is a memory
Passed down to the children
Only to be reminded of the past

A resemblance of reputation held closed
Among acquaintance far and near
All is but now a book opened to the slipping past

[67] Naturally awesome

The rule of nature
The sun, the moon and the stars
Ruling by the day and night
Above the mighty sky
Above the raging seas

The tides
Bring life to the sea
The experience
Awesomely written
Magnificently demonstrated

A conquest
A routine
Challenges each breath
In the newness of time
Like clichés

This is life
This is a bargain
To every breathing creature
They are part of nature

We share, we glimpse
The proof of creation
Inspiring
Exuberant
Wonderful feelings
Appreciating the exhibits

The rainbow wraps it all
The promise of life
The promise of hope
As we gaze adorably
The endless beauty
Of all seasons and time

[68] Prayer

Prayer calls
A time to seek
The blessings of unconditional love
Only the humble can make it plain

Prayer calls
The seeking heart to rest
The gift of peace and solace sought
Evidently discharged right away to the distress call

Prayer calls
The mountains will be removed
Faith increases and self-dominance decreases
All for wonders to be revered even night falls

[69] Realize it

No one appreciates sorrow
It depreciates the value of life
Let me dwell in the peace of my mind
My solace for a restful heart

No one appreciates losses
Especially the loss of a loved one
Time has bound us in understanding each other
Till the bond is broken, now only a written memory remains

No one appreciates love unwritten
Confessed love in action is not seen as evidence
Until it's gone and now I have to do it all alone
Past demonstrations of love, now I treasure them the most

[70] Resolution

Remember every moment of the days ahead
Each promise made and the dreams that follow
Such is a noble dream that will see us through

Over troubled waters of the ocean blue waves
Laboring to defeat the forces of nature's rage
Until the clear skies reign the atmosphere again

Tearing all doubts that dreams are dreams unattainable
Instead great dreams make great people dream bigger dreams
Only the courageous with a firm mind and heart will confess
Never admit defeat, the fall to realizing dreams so lovely
    and true

[71] Sacrifice

When our beloved spouse is down
Not in health
In need of a helping hand
Will we be there?
To comfort, to assure?

Live to the vow
In sickness and in health
Fulfilling it—the greatest honor
Commitments and love rekindled
A sacrifice, much and truly cherished

Reach out and witness the regeneration
A long lasting impression revived
The bonding enhanced
Recipe to restore intimacy
No wealth or health can ever contest
In exchange for love so pure and defined

[72] Satisfaction

Satisfaction is a matter of soul over mind
The will power over the intellect
And the emotion must be fairly played too
No complete satisfaction can ever rule the soul

When satisfaction is not clearly defined
Satisfaction is when I have the things I want done my way
Or satisfaction is when I feel free to do what I want
Or satisfaction is when boredom is no longer embedded

But removed for good and not in the thought anymore
Or satisfaction is simply doing what pleases others more
Above our own satisfaction and standards
Whatever the interpretation is

Are you happy in the end?
Got what you want and are others happy too?
Not simply others who take advantage
But those called our loved ones and beloved too

Immeasurable it is to say
Satisfaction is only a feeling
The mind can never understand
Only those who treasure will be able to

Looking back
Reflecting on the surprising moments
Crazy they can be but all is well
When it's meant to be well

[73] Say it

When you're down
Just say you need words of comfort
Words that won't drift to heal
But words that are sincerely expressed
Exhaled through hearts that feel

When you're exhausted
Just say you need a little time for yourself
The little time to recuperate
But rest with a free mind
Arresting the moments of unimagined fatigue

When you're joyful
Just cheer another soul
The little cheer is worth every second
But cheer with the simplest sincerity
Making hearts touched and hope renewed

When you're feeling on top of the world
Just enjoy the free air that you breathe
The air that keeps everything and everyone hale
But rise to the occasion when it's threatened and polluted
For the air we breathe is akin to a borrowed world from
    our children

[74] Shout it out loud

Let the mountains know it's summer
Let the sheep hear the voice of the shepherd
Let the rivers flow to the deepest ocean
Let the fish swim willfully across all depths

If mountains, sheep, rivers and the fish can do wonders
Man can do better
It's all in the mind
The emotion controls all actions
The intellect boasts all knowledge subdued over time
While the will can only direct the submissive heart

Get real and learn to do it right
All things will gloriously fall into place
The mindset, the beliefs and the lifestyle
All will have to submit and be in line
Just to be steamed and catapulted to victory

See it, know it and believe it
You'll see
You'll be amazed
That's the victory
Shout it out loud

[75] Sincerity

Thank you
The common expression
Lost its impression
Many have lost patience
Saying it is a loss
Really how could it be?
It means everything
Just live with it
You'll be glad
You have said it

Please is another
So courteous you have been
Many have forgotten
The magic word that arrests the soul
It's not popular but a must
Promotes respect in all

You are welcome, another great note
Teaches us to stay low
Responding in appreciation
Grateful we should be
The value that creates
Nobility among the respected

I am sorry
Not my cup of tea
Don't drive me up the walls
It's just not me
Why should I—I am clean
Insisting, I'll say it
A connotation, many don't really mean

Thank you
Please
You are welcome
I am sorry
Not to beg but make it right
Beat the odds and you'll be glad

[76] Sleep tight

The clock chimes
At the stroke of midnight
It's time to declare rest
Forget the pain
Forget the strain
Forget the forlorn emotions
Shows of vanity

Dream sweet in the cool midnight breeze
Sweet dreams will remain gratifying as honey
Catching up with the lost time of deep rest
Seasoned with lovely, adorable thoughts
Blooming flowers seem white satins in display
Filling the meadow as far as the eyes can behold
Seemingly beauty in display slowly fading into the misty air

I will be awake soon
Let me continue and rise feeling excited
My request for excitement is not mine to command
My desire is mine to rest
Addressing setbacks will be tomorrow's care
The beauty of my sleep none can ever compare
Only the still, small whispers at dawn will be my light

Sunrise will be another day to stay
The crow of the cockerel signals the very day
Pick up the usual and keep the flaws at bay
As the proverb "make hay" strongly conveys
Another great day it has been set to be
Zestful thinking caressing the whole day
My sleep, my dream is here to stay

[77] Song of passion

Sing it loud
Let the whole world hear it
Rhythm and melody
Singing alive the hope there is

Secrets they convey
Illustrations of beauty
Splendidly phrased
Appealing, entertaining

Each line tinkles sweet
Swinging mood leaving
And now arise the new beginning
Leading the way

Breaking emotional blues
Stinging but now blooming
Displaying grace and love
Incredible, unbelievable

[78] Stay sober

What's the matter?
Wondering and thinking so hard?
Has hope lost its horizon?
Surely that's an illusion
A play of the mind
Entertain not
This isn't a play

We may be on stage
Where emotions sway
Minds get weary
Though it's really unnecessary
Thinking hope is gone
And opportunities thinning away
Behold, believe and submit not
The illusion is just temporary

It's not here to stay
Unless, you've opened the way
The way to destruction it is
So, claim your way
Stay strong and calm
Your weapon and shield
None can ever claim theirs
Cos' they're rightfully yours

[79] Stay strong

Everything matters
Big and small, they'll still do
Think not too seriously of things so mundane
Feeling upset drives us deeper into depression
Feeling confused pushes us down the walkway

Whatever the feeling is, bottle it up not
It's destruction to the self
Feeling jilted and unloved
Believe that the little gift you have
Small and unimportant it may seem
It's actually meant for you to be
Cos' you're special in your own way

Nobody will ever understand it
The truth will reveal itself
Your absence will make others long for you
Even your critics will look up to you
The belief—we complement each other much
Unfortunately, it's often overlooked
The pain of being unnoticed and unlisted

No matter what happens
You are still yourself
Keep your head held high
The ultimate survival key
To stay afloat above all odds
Knowing we choose our paths and destiny
And nobody can ever take that away, forever!

[80] Stop it!

Stop the massacre
The insane genocide
None will approve
A human with conscience will never take side

Can't you hear their cries?
Can't you hear their pleas?
They are your brothers and your sisters
They are your mothers and your fathers

Be in their shoes, pleading for mercy
Be in their situation, mercilessly ridiculed
Have we lost our senses?
Have we lost our directions?

Return to the path
A path that shows love for our fellow man
Reaching out our hands to deliver them
The cries will stop

Sounds of rejoicing will fill the air
Once again, life spared is life celebrated
Another day spared, nothing's certain anymore
Will there be sunrise tomorrow for me to see?
Will there be sounds of grace ringing the streets
The moment has come
Make it come and bless the day!

[81] Stories of love

Love
It's not lost and a pain
It's been there all this while
Unrecognized of its existence
Exhaustion
Anger
Depression
Poor man's judgment
The genesis of all miseries
Fallen nature of man

Love
It's not lost and silent
Launch it into the deep
Let love be a song
A song that hums melodies of delight
Delightful hearts rise from the core
To the stars above
Glistening in the twilight
Drowning multiple hurts and ill-feelings
The pain is forgotten now—diminishing

Love
It's not lost and forbidden
The best ever planned connection between man
Nuptials tied deep down the innermost
Forgiving, entertaining are its sacrifices
The sacrifice not many can easily identify
Immeasurable sacrifices known only to earnest givers

[82] Survival rules

Pressing others down to move up
Another cliché?
Asking others to listen
A welcomed liberty?
Forcing others to do the opposite
An encroachment?
Abusing others for pleasure
A sadist in style?

The saddest of all is . . .
When we lose sight of our relations
I, me and myself and no one else
The first rule of survival cuts off humanity
The world is never for us
To press others down
To dictate others to listen
To force others against their will
And to take pleasure in seeing others suffer

Rather, survival is equal opportunity
Opportunists have never reckoned
What's mine is destined for me
To seize what I can take and reign
Sufferings of others are not mine to care
I've got my share, now it's fairer to share
Bridging the gap, I'll not partake
I'll continue doing what it takes
After all, life is only a moment in time

The moment will come
All is gone but what remains will only be
Memories of what's done
None of what is owned
So please, let's care
Make the world a better place
Welcomed for all

[83] Teach me

I am all weak
To show I am independent
Able to do things on my own
And be glad I've done it

I am all nervous
To stand before a crowd and speak
Speaking my mind and sincere thoughts
And feel good I've overcome my inferiority

I am all afraid
To reveal my gifts of love
Love that will be taken for granted
Creating a loss of my self-worth

I am all oblivion to change
To notice the blessings before me
Taking me step after step of faith
Breaking me and restoring me whole

Obsession is to blame
Let it not reign
Our only hope
Delivered forever

[84] Teacher

A teacher is born, not made
The service rendered isn't a trade
Neither will it degrade and fade
A heritage it will be until life turns into hate

Be of good courage and continue to fight on
You'll never know when to stop calling it fond
Gracious you have been, cheer on and on
That's the strength to hold and move on

Bad memories, put them aside
These are flickers that make you a knight
Bear the peace and display not the angry side
Victorious you will be, but pride not in thy might

All that begins well will surely end well
The sacrifices have been compensated well
Take pride in your stride as you learn to dwell
The end will be all taken care of, it will not be a living hell

[85] Tell me

Motorcycles in a motorcade
Taking half the road
Safety not a criteria
King of the road in range
Poor mentality of the indifferent
Graze them and a commotion is sure
Beaten up and harsh words entail
Careful or not, always not their fault at all

Ruthless, ruthless motorcyclists
Motorists not an exception too
Overtaking from the left a norm now
Minor bangs can turn ugly
The careful ones often stared
Confused, not able to understand
Why, a generation so rude and uncivilized

Tell me
Drivers' incompetence?
Instructors' ingenuity?
Roads turned into graves
Safety no longer a concern
In a hurry I am

Who cares? Lives are at threat
Children left without guardians
The innocent left without limbs and sight
The unbearable ones—collapse on the spot
Gone but in memory remains

[86] The amazing life

Look around
Everything speaks
We become the subject
Conversations bring insights
People see much in us
We don't really identify well

Have we ever asked ourselves?
Why have others spoken about us?
Have they complained about our conversations?
Have they been taken offence by our acts?
Have they considered our feelings?
Rather, have we considered their feelings too?

Complain no more
Grow and live by the standards
They are the means to stand tall
Walking and standing tall with the rest
They too walk the same dusty roads
The same will qualify us
To be acceptable by the set standards

Speak and participate in no evil
Nasty conversations and acts
Are but a game of the ungrateful
Seeking justice for the self
Sidelining others is their survival
Keep to the standard
We will see the best coming
The best bargains knocking on our doors

Be still and know
Deep down within
Springs the wells of life
Rivers of hope
Rivers of good returns
None can ever conceive the promises
Of the everlasting arms of life's bliss

[87] The climb

The highest peak I've ever climbed
My life at 20, I did it all
Awesome view above the firmaments
Trees, now turned to shrubs, donned the sides

The natives are so strong
Ladies at 70, carrying gas above
Can we imagine doing it?
We'll fall before we know it

Sunrise was a beautiful scene
Too picturesque, words can't describe
Lovely thought, amazing feelings
A conqueror of it, now a picture of contentment

Again another ascend is beyond belief
At 26, before I left the Land Below the Wind
Satisfied, amazed at my victory
An experience, engraved in thought

[88] The curse of sin

Wickedness rules
Careless lives become a scene
No feelings of guilt
No repentance
Why not?
Look around
Can't you see?
Everybody's doing it

It's beyond conviction
The conscience is dead
The will no longer rules
The emotions say "I will submit"
The mind says "It's okay"
The sense of direction
Lost and never found

The curse of sin
The plague of misery
The destruction of mankind
Babies dumped everywhere
By the doorsteps
In the dustbins
In toilet bowls
Bushes are not spared

It's becoming a disease
Backstabbing's becoming a game
Slithering tongues spread the curse
Joyful sounds shout the lines
Serve you right
You started it first
Feel it and die in it

Life's journey is never intended to be so
Majestic it will be
Destined to rule over
Not otherwise—ruled by sin
Know this . . . the truth

Death to the soul is life to a destiny
The beginning of a new hope
The renewal of the mind
The ultimate escape
To eternal bliss forever

[89] The deception

Perception can be a deception
Deceiving trusting hearts
Relinquishing opportunities
Time can never buy

Save the soul
Save what not
Unnecessary worries
We often look for

Stop looking for them
They will come
Just act naive but be vigilant
The shield that never fails

Beliefs are common
Until they are acted on
Stay sound and you'll be fine
Nothing can wildly creep
Until we become negligent
The opening that sets the destruction

Keep shielding
Stay on course
The only armor
From the costly deceptive moment

[90] The gift

Writing my thoughts
One fine gift I've never thought
Will I be a blessing?
Encouraging a soul to strength
Will I bring cheer?
Making another face smile broadly
Will I bring the hope?
Leading the way for a seeking heart

Let the heart's desire be revealed
Make known of all noble intentions
Life's purpose and directions
All for one resolution
Free from condemnation
Justified, all from one revelation

Arise
Let not the moment pass
For conscience sake
One opportunity is one decision
Above all the wisdom of man
All from a noble call
The greatest gift of words to share

[91] The land of a thousand smiles

Look around the world
Places people go and stay
But my Historical State of Melaka
Great bargains and smiles you'll find here

Awesome, friendly people you'll meet
A conversation struck, memories will retain
Smiles stream down innocent faces
Welcoming every soul, it's been ages

A home of smiles,
Meant for everybody
The resounding snores
Lovely and enjoyed the most

Call it an island, we have plenty of them
Delicacies and cuisines, a pleasure enjoyed the most
Highlands and golf courses have been great attractions
Only the affluent rich can say it's worth it

Smile, my Melaka State
Your popularity is unmatchable
March on in the spirit of democracy
Your publicity is our prosperity

[92] The masterpiece

Love
The masterpiece of the Almighty
His love never ceases
His love never fails
His love never grows old
His love is evergreen

Mercy
His mercy is never exhaustive
His mercy is never a shame
His mercy is never a weakness
His mercy is never lacking
His mercy is everlasting

Grace
His grace is forever new
His grace is eternally available
His grace is free to trade
His grace is more than sufficient
His grace is His and His alone

Think about us
Do we have all these?
Love, mercy and grace
Desire these gifts
Trade everything for these
We'll be different
Purposeful and meaningful
Life will be

[93] The modern day challenge

Ever pondered in depth?
Mobile phones ringing
People texting and talking
Even drivers die chatting

Children are not spared
Teenagers craze for new apps
Willing to trade for one
For anything it will cost, really?

Parents, set the conditions
Nothing should come free
Education first? Attitude change?
Insist on them and trade accordingly

TVs and computers
Equal damages done in time
Oversee their use
They are like the roars of the ocean deep
Sinking even the mighty and humble give in

Stop it
It's like the flood
None will survive
Submerged and hopes lost
By the craze and technology invasion

[94] The optimist

Morning breakfast—is there any?
None as usual, a whisper from deep within
O dear, another difficult morning
Probably, no lunch and dinner too
A dinner will do if no lunch is available

I must be strong
I must be persistent
I must be brave
I must learn . . .
To stretch forth my arms
Whisper a word of thanks
A word of comfort

There will be a kind soul coming
He will notice me
There'll be something
I'll stay alive for yet another while

The birds can sing melodiously
The sweet sounds of life is a cheer
It's okay
I'll be okay

The birds are happy
I'll be happy
Just as the past has been
I'll not go hungry
There'll be something soon

[95] The pursuit

Enough is enough of every day grouses
Still complaining?
A common game it is

A satisfied life is in the mind
A life that has everything
Something that hurts many

Satisfaction is just an empty pursuit
Greed has overcome many
Wrestle not with it
It's not worth pursuing
Even dying for

Lacking something isn't the end
It's something to treasure
The things we already have
Enjoying them every day
Let pursuits be realistic

Play not the game of the heart
Vanity may rule
But we have the upper hand

Worry not
It's destined
We learn through great pains

Precept by precept they will be
Painful lessons they may be
Experience the lessons and grow
Maturing us to appreciate

Simple life is great life
Pursue it

[96] The reward of patience

Steer close to reality
A small mistake takes the fall
Safety crosses the soul
If not careful, misery will crawl

On the road, all else matter
Not our safety alone to care
Remember those at home
Waiting at the door, let them wail not

Let the old self die to where it belongs
Let the spirit live above all cries
The misery and authority we spread
All unto a good cause after all

A minute earlier doesn't make matters better
Instead, crawl along if you need
Red and green lights are clear to obey
Our way is not steered out to our dismay

[97] The treasure

Friends of all shapes and sizes
Friends of all characters and behaviors
Friends of many makes
They make life a wonder to stay

True friends come in silent sent
Opportune ones take a step ahead
To lend a hand is a thousand curse
Mostly a betrayal in shadow plays

True acquaintance a rare glimpse
Subtle they come to care
Reaching out and touching gently
Their presence is but a colorful array

Love and care, their shine displays life
Their presence silences souls to the ground
None can claim and declare
I've done it all for a friend's sake

[98] The unforgettable beauty

Have they not been around
Silence will rule our every sidewalk
The sound and noise of their presence
Enlivens every sleepy hollow
The time they rise,
Life begins as the birds tweet happily
Approving the start of life again

Darkest nights, now turned to day
Bringing unsinkable joy
Sounds of music fill the air
Spicing up excited living souls all their might
Every brook now a hive of activities
The gift of life with no recognizable boundaries
With children noisily shouting amplified to their larynx

Beautiful as they gracefully flow
Children diving excitedly
Noticeably fearless of nothing
Gracefully canoeing along
Feeling unbound now,
It's the weekend
Not a siesta, but literally a fiesta outdoor
The escape after a hard-pressed week

The scenic beauty
Mesmerizes grinning nature lovers
Appealing much to morning strollers
Joining the momentous laughter
Coming from the refreshed faces upstream
Keep it that way to serenade every soulful creature
Let us therefore sustain the natural ,
Just for the children's sake and their generation
Let's do it together, living on their borrowed time

[99] The untamed need

Friendship is mutual
Built not on stilts but consensual
Like it, continue as usual
Be mature and responsible

Water it and be faithful
The bloom will be a school
Colorful and magnificently cool
Like a swimming pool

Call it a big fame
Grandeur is its name
It may be sometimes a game
Shame it will be if untamed

Create a long-lasting one
Until the day is done
It is a gate to all fun
Treasured next to none

Believe me
Friends are for free
But they are like a tree
Sturdy, growing without a plea

[100] There's time

There's time for everything
Doing something casual just to see the time pass
Meaningful some can be
To remember and to search the soul
The heart and mind are neither spared though

There's time for the self
Studying and learning to live my life to the fullest
Life's experiences are life's maturing resources
Playing, enjoying and discovering my potentials
That I may serve to my best and be blest

There's time for the family
A sacrifice so great, immeasurable to repay
The least I can say, I'll do what I may
To care and play my role as child to cheer and pray
That I'll be a giver of life and see the lives of my beloved
    sustained

There's time for my country
That I'll not ask what my country can do for me
Instead, I'll ask what I can do for my country,
Sharing the sentiment of a great leader of the west
Making sure that I'm here to beget peace and love forever

[101] Time for action

The crave of man is super fantastic
Every crave calls for a reflection
Let's evaluate

A mansion?
When there are those enjoying only the open sky as their
    roofs
A luxurious car?
When the dusty roads are filled with those still walking in
    slippers
A promotion?
When a menial task is a heavy burden
A more lucrative income?
When the jobless are still struggling making ends meet
A more sumptuous meal?
When another table is void of the basic
Designer clothes?
When many don't even have decent clothes to cover them
A more understanding friend?
When opportunists outnumbered the true ones
Better of everything?
When too much of everything is nothing
But an unwelcomed destruction
Knocking on the door
Striking hard when the time is up

Many have forgotten
The blessings of aplenty is to be kind
Share with those in want
Meet the simplest desires of the wanting soul
Stretch forth caring hands and touch one
Create lovelier sisterhood and brotherhood bonds
Make sharing an equity of love
Reach out, give hope and a better destiny to the needy
Cheering smiles will be a scene so splendid to behold
More than wealth and pseudo-happiness can offer

[102] Time matters

It takes time to love
Somebody new especially
Caution however
Many are on the prowl
Looking for easy preys

It takes time to sacrifice
The things so dear to us
Note however
No sacrifice no returns
A blessing is on the way

It takes time to realize
The events in our lives
People come and go
Like angels whispering the hope
A hope of life later on the beautiful shore

It takes time to change
Ponder upon every moment
Good moments enlighten
Ugly times break the moment
Break free before the crucial time expires

[103] Track on

Complaints are so common
They are nothing but a thorn in the flesh
Instead turn complaints into compliments
See the change they bring
Amazing hope and smiles are now a game to play

A life of denial is no longer safe
It eats into the deeper parts of the bones
And breaks all assurance and confidence
Beat it and move on anew
Dwell no more in it but scramble
Lest the conscience so pure is consumed

Words of compliments have become a cliché
Uplifting they may seem to unsuspecting souls
Like roaring lions they come and stay
The influence we will unwillingly submit
Breaking the feelings of despair
Many have fallen victims, wounded and angry
Keep moving there is still life left to move on

Believe me
Nothing is a co-incidence
Everything that happens is planned
Bad plans destroy trust and harmony
Good plans nourish the spirit, soul and body
Keep on your guard and know nothing is a fair play
The assurance may be astounding but it's really a shadow
Keep everything at bay lest weariness will stay and keep us
    at play

[104] Wake up

True friends are a gem, really
They'll stand by us
Take them not for granted
They are God-sent

True moments are life's lessons
They reveal realities we despise
Learn from them with interest
They'll rescue us from further falls

True satisfaction is a dream
Even the rich is not satisfied
Slow to realize many are in want
Only when they become one
Repentance comes

[105] When I talk

When I talk so much, I'm called "talkative"
When I'm dead quiet, I'm accused of being dumb
When I share my two cents worth of opinion,
They say I'm showing off
When will people learn?
To stop accusing
Playing with sentiments
The very depths of our sensitive soul
Breaking our true being
Created with dignity and a sense of pride

Are they ignorant, not to know
That silence can mean being in deep thoughts
Not to offend but are they clowning around
With the immature show of disrespect?
Not sensing the importance and urgency
The heartfelt words of sincerity is ours to behold
The moment the mouth speaks
Every possible condemnation starts to take its course
None is so comfortable listening without speaking back

Verbal reflex as I would call
A bad norm, badly designed
Enmity pursues and subdues
Souls confused to the brim through penetrable firewalls
Reality announces its authority
None can beat it, only we
Till the last breath of life we breathe
Down the aisle of death

[106] While I'm here

Look for me when I'm still around
There'll be sorrows treated to a mountain dew
There'll be joys indescribable, unimaginable
Beyond the clear skies
Beyond the horizon
Beyond the meadows
Where you'll grow wings like eagles
Wings that help soar above the mightiest wind
Wings that effortlessly conquer all the might there is
Wings that know no failure
Wings that flap not like the sparrows
But wings that generate confidence and trust
Overtaking unpredictable situations that come and go
Soar like an eagle
Above all the odds of life

When I'm no longer to be found, it'll be a different story
Will I be missed?
Will I be words of comfort?
To them who live in solitude
Will they remember me?
I was once like them
Shackled and lost
I found my strength renewed
A new flow of might every morning
That keeps me soar above my feelings
Keeping a balance of joy and harmony
Trickling like dripping water from stalactites
Molding new creations
Giving nature a new beauty
Gazed and admired

Till everything takes shape and later dies
Kept and remembered only in snapshots
A token for life it will be
Another token kept in the album
Joining those in past lineage
Encrypted and carved in wax
Remembered but not for long
For I will only be
Another memorabilia in collection

[107] Why is it so hard?

The first time I said I care
You doubted my caring attitude
The second time I said I would love you till the end
You doubted my deepest sincerity
The third time I said I would support you wholeheartedly
You doubted my pure intentions

Why is so hard to believe?
Was there a time I hurt your feelings?
I'm sorry if I had
Was there a time I made you doubt me?
Believe me
Many things have changed
Ever since that day
The day I promised myself

This is a new beginning
The moment that means everything to me
Walk with me as I hold your hands
Through this journey where bliss is on our side
The hope that will stay forever
Till the clock stops its chime of life

Note:
Expressions like this need not be for the poet. It's more to reach out
to different readers who may have experienced similar situations—
thus, the hope for reconciliation is much wished for so that the life
built on mutual trust will continue to flourish over time.

[108] Would you be there?

Lay not a hand on it
If you are not willing
Stay afar off the coast
Show not your face
Feeling unwelcomed is okay
Remember this is not your day

Seasons come and go
Play your game safe
Know who is game for it
Don't force it, nobody likes it
Not even me
Take it and leave

But know how the game is played
Be willing and available
You'll see the difference
You'll make the difference
It all starts with us
Steer close to the coast
You'll be noticed and loved

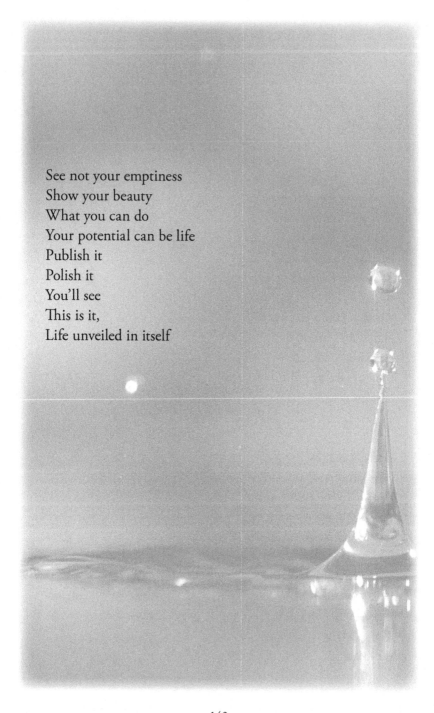

See not your emptiness
Show your beauty
What you can do
Your potential can be life
Publish it
Polish it
You'll see
This is it,
Life unveiled in itself

[109] You're born a victor

What more can I say? It's done
Shakespeare's "What's done can't be undone" stays
Every fault is all-noticed
Every help rendered is all-expected
Do we owe anyone anything?
If there is, this is it
Know it right away

Words tell more than feelings bottled up
Let them pour and let tears tear down every barrier
We need to grow and keep growing
Stunted growth, held down is detrimental
Stay afloat above all
You'll be amazed
There's so much to live for

Stay above the roars of the ocean
And still the anger of the storm
They may come but remember, we are in control
Lose it not
That's our victory
The victory is sweet, sway not

The victory is already won
Thus, be not deceived
Never let guilt and fault rule
We are no longer naive
Only the playful and calculative will
The destruction, so-uninviting will play on

[110] Yours truly

Confess "I care" as often as you can
Its appreciation is beyond description
Imagine saying it to one lost soul, searching for solace
The words would mean a thousand sounds of hope
Healing every pain and misery ever imagined

Articulate it and work on it
You'll never understand the measures that will unfold
You'll be blessed
Your coming in and going out will be a mystery revealed
Like the Pandora Box, revealing the unbelievable

Secrets of the thousand hills, none can ever comprehend
Take heart, however and know
Sad hearts appreciate it most
Say it truthfully and the return is far-fetched
The light is liberated so freely that illness will just be
    health

A little sacrifice of whatever it can be
And the gift of encouragement will surely and truly
Change lives and life's perspective
That it's greater to bless than to demand
Akin to giving than receiving
Love is all meaningful when shared
Keep sharing and you'll be receiving!

BONUS READING
for
PERSONAL
REFLECTIONS

[B1] The inevitable change

Our past
A collection of memories and lessons
Filled with good and heart-arresting events
Lives changed in seconds

Repentance
A change for the better
Characters improved to nobility
Pride miraculously turned into humility

Eternal grudge and hate to eternal love
Nothing remains unchanged forever
One slight mistake can change good perceptions
One good deed will not promise otherwise

The lessons are great
Evaluate every encounter
The choice will hopefully uphold us
Memories will remain etched

But a new man will be born
Pretty on the outward, beautiful inward
A change in life dimension
Bringing strengths and new hopes
For another day of confession and pleasure

Synopsis 1

We have lots of past memories that are both pleasant and unforgettably mind-boggling. Nevertheless, we need to learn to rise above all circumstances that have made miseries haunt us and driven us up the walls. Life has to move on despite bitterness and other mountains of dissatisfactions that might drown us into despair.

We can't easily make people realize and repent of their wrongdoings, whether on purpose or otherwise. Some just need more time to recognize and learn from their mistakes. There's none perfect, even among the great men in the past. Subconsciously, we may have enmity with our best of friends and colleagues but holding them back in grudge will not improve any situation. Instead, we are putting ourselves in bound as the first rule to change is to "Release it freely" and we will then experience the liberty.

Each encounter in life is a lesson to mature us so that we will be more streetwise and know that life is all about making the right choice to avert future regrets and needless heart—breaking moments.

Change is said to be the fundamental of human progress which no one can ever deny. The change of attitude builds character and the change of character will lead to improved personality. Change is unavoidable, yet needful.

[B2] The touch

Unbearable falls
Hurting within
Crushed to the ground
Unfeeling pain dominates

Anger takes precedence
Controlling the inner man
Fight on
The battle must be won

Whatsoever the cost
No regrets
Linger no longer
Get over the resentment

The downfall of man
Steer clear to the light
Shadow plays cloud the mind
Be in control

New hope, new beginning
Bad trails left behind
The awaited deliverance
Now, be still and calm

Justice prevails!

Synopsis 2

A fall is a pain to the skin that takes time to recuperate, especially one that involves challenging one's integrity and invading another person's privacy. In effect, anger rolls out of nowhere in retaliation, no matter what the consequence may be.

Soberness must play along and reassess the situation. The Psalmist forewarns of confrontations as they who refuse to budge and learn will retaliate in response to advice, viewed as threats. These shall soon be cut down like the grass and wither as the green herb. Thus, staying on course and not shadow-play situations would be the wisest of all wisdom.

Offsetting precarious situations with God-given wisdom is best done to deliver ourselves from superfluous attack of the personality and name-smearing schemes. It takes us to look into and analyze all situations before engaging in emotional plays and acting like someone sane, while in actual truth we are only endangering the self with more of other unwelcomed guiles of the enemy. Justice will prevail.

[B3] Roles undefined

The chair
A representation of authority
Instructing and overseeing
Appreciating capabilities
Rewarding justly with credibility
Blessings, flowing like never ending streams

Character
Akin to a sturdy tree
Built on a firm foundation
Nothing can ever move it
Not even the storm or flood
Unperturbed by threats and silent melodies

Reputation
A distorted shadow with no purity
Like the morning dew
Diminishing into thin air
Its might plundered
A temporary habitation

Valor,
A bridge to victory
The breastplate of faith
Mightier than the sword
Assurance of triumph in uncertainties
Uncontested to its demise

Synopsis 3

"Roles undefined" is written based on the reality of hierarchical practice and dominion in the society. It's so unfortunate that though work quality and undivided sacrifice are rendered without question, the game of ignorance and foul play have become widespread like wildfire. Positions have incessantly taken precedence over fair execution of duty and dominated the carnal mind. Conditional cliques and probably fame are now a battle ground for many.

Character is expected in effective leadership. When respect is due, it will be freely given with no reservations. Nevertheless, character that is akin to a sturdy tree does not easily fall in those with clear life principles. No nonsense is a game to consider and play at all.

On the other hand, reputation is earned, and not forced. It's a nobility to be reputed among allies and foes alike. Backstabbing is not soon forthcoming until the self gives in to pride and self-destruction. It may become the prized badge that only one fall will bring in the unanticipated disaster.

Valor is part of the entire game too. Stand up in defense of truth and do not compromise on values as cronyism has perpetuated detrimental effects on God-fearing souls. Living up to audacity will certainly bring forth the optimism for justice to ensue until its demise.

[B4] Give meaning to life

Troubles come and go
Hidden messages to mature
Challenges to beat and become victorious
Victory matters

Blessings known and unknown
Our comfort in times of despair
Knowing many lie in streets
Not to mention the threats of death
Churning stomachs begging for mercy

Empathy outgrows Sympathy
People have lost the touch
Hunger and thirst devouring
Feeble bodies but determined
To battle on till the last

Synopsis 4

Life without pain is void of appreciation. As life's journey is packed with diverse and a multitude of painful experiences, they are, however, the essentials of maturity where we learn to outlive tragedies and grief that make us stoop so low as if life is a predestined journey that no one can amend. Before the closing of our chapter, the battle must be well fought because victory will lean to our side as we press on.

The quote "Life is a song—sing it. Life is a game—play it. Life is a challenge—meet it. Life is a dream—realize it. Life is a sacrifice—offer it. Life is love—enjoy it" by Sai Baba clearly illustrates that life is a wonderfully designed assortment of choice given to all. Thus, life deserves all the prospects we need in making every ground that we tread an opportunity towards realizing the dream.

Many have suffered through numerous difficult times, beyond description, even to the verge of giving up and questioning if life is really fair. Empathy must be advocated over sympathy to revive the human touch and the spirit of humanity.

I would like to share an adage by Sholom leichem that discloses "Life is a dream for the wise, a game for the fool, a comedy for the rich, a tragedy for the poor." It's indisputably true that life is well-lived when we take all the vigilant steps in breathing into life the quintessence it deserves.

[B5] A time to appreciate

My very own flesh and blood in motion
A lovely thing to behold and sing
The source of my soul and inspiration
The keeper of my well-being

Thank you for being there
Making life a comfort to cope
Ensuring that I am not left bare
Giving life a lovely hope

The very reason to celebrate
Careful strides that will shade
To stay afloat and ahead
Forgetting not the unselfish trade

Look ahead and stay great
Leave not this journey to fate
Life together makes life great
Leave not a room to sow hate

Let's keep life going
As it has always been
Making life spring
Keeping the feeble and strong keen

We are a FAMILY
Father And Mother, I Love You!

Synopsis 5

Our God-given parents are unquestionably irreplaceable and incomparable gifts. They were there to witness and welcome our entry into this wonderful creation with hearts that can never be explained. They have led us through the thick and thin of life. They protected us to ensure that we are not ill-treated and condemned without defense.

Being wonderfully fashioned, we were taught to love, care and be responsible towards ourselves, siblings, parents and friends alike. Their concern has never been compromised, resembling the fishermen's determination not to return empty handed at the end of their toil at sea.

Indeed, they have been the keeper of our well-being and the source of our inspiration. Nothing that we do can ever contest and recompense their tireless sacrifices. That's the type of life we are to render, just the same, to our children and children's children as they see the wonders of life as envisioned. Nonetheless, the best lesson to teach is to help them soar and stay ahead volatile situations that are without doubt forthcoming.

The greatest of all is none other than their tireless effort in making life great and as meaningful as it can be. Appreciate them for as long as they are there to lend a hand and be noticed of their presence. As parents-to-be in the near future, we might also expect a similar or probably a better treatment from our children, as much as we have played our part as loving and caring parents.

Stay great and make life great and going.